A Guide to

BRITAIN and IRELAND

Kevin Pettman

WAYLAND
www.waylandbooks.co.uk

Published in 2018 in paperback by Wayland
Copyright © Hodder and Stoughton, 2017

Written by Kevin Pettman
Interior design by Simon Letchford
Cover design by Pete Clayman
Edited by Corinne Lucas

ISBN: 978 1 5263 6031 1

Wayland, an imprint of
Hachette Children's Group
Part of Hodder and Stoughton
Carmelite House
50 Victoria Embankment
London EC4Y 0DZ

An Hachette UK Company
www.hachette.co.uk
www.hachettechildrens.co.uk

MIX
Paper from responsible sources
FSC® C104740
FSC
www.fsc.org

Printed in China
10 9 8 7 6 5 4 3 2 1

Contents

Welcome to Britain and Ireland

From cups of tea and wet weather to ancient history and modern sculpture, England, Wales, Scotland, Northern Ireland and the Republic of Ireland, may make up a small group of islands but they're bursting with facts …

 England

Population: 54 million (approximately)

Capital city: London

 Scotland

Population: 5.3 million

Capital city: Edinburgh

 Republic of Ireland

Population: 4.6 million

Capital city: Dublin

 **Wales**

Population: 3.1 million

Capital city: Cardiff

 Northern Ireland

Population: 1.8 million

Capital city: Belfast

Great Britain = England, Wales and Scotland.

UK (United Kingdom) = England, Wales, Scotland and Northern Ireland.

United Kingdom and Republic of Ireland = England, Wales, Scotland, Northern Ireland and Republic of Ireland.

There are more than **5,000 islands** around the coast and seas of Britain and Ireland.

The ancient **Book of Kells** is a religious manuscript that's over 1,200 years old. It's on display at Trinity College Dublin (see page 44).

The **Giant's Causeway** in Northern Ireland has about 40,000 interlocking rock columns. It was created by a volcanic eruption nearly 60 million years ago (see page 33).

The famous **RMS *Titanic*** ship, which was 269 metres long and weighed 46,000 tonnes, was built in Belfast between 1909 and 1912 (see page 60).

 The **smallest house** in Britain and Ireland is just 1.82 metres wide and 2.84 metres high. It is in Conwy in north Wales (see page 38).

The **lowest point** in Britain and Ireland is North Slob in County Wexford, Republic of Ireland, which is 3 metres below sea level (see page 55).

 Famous children's author **Roald Dahl** was born in Cardiff in 1916. Dahl was also a fighter pilot during the Second World War (see page 45).

 Land's End in Cornwall is the most westerly point in England. There are 130 recorded shipwrecks around its rocks (see page 32).

The **Calanais Standing Stones** on the Isle of Lewis are thought to be around 5,000 years old (see page 50).

Ben Nevis is the highest mountain in Britain and Ireland at 1,346 metres above sea level. Around 100,000 people climb it each year (see page 54).

Edinburgh Castle in central Scotland, was first built in the 12th century. It sits on Castle Rock, which was formed from a volcano about 350 million years ago (see page 41).

The *Angel of the North* is a giant steel sculpture that's 54 metres wide. It was unveiled in 1998 and stands on a hill near Gateshead (see page 11).

The **Grand Union** canal is 220-kilometres long and runs from Birmingham to London (see page 48).

London is the **biggest city** within these islands, with more than 8.6 million people living there. Famous landmarks include the Houses of Parliament, London Eye and Big Ben (see page 41).

Queen Victoria died in 1901, at Osborne House on the Isle of Wight (see page 38).

Great dates

Britain and Ireland may be small compared to other countries, but they have a long and interesting timeline. Take a look at these dates to brush up on your history.

5,000 BCE

In 5,000 BCE, people are still using stone tools and are **hunter-gatherers**. This means they hunt for food and gather plants.

2,500 BCE

Farming largely replaces hunting and gathering by 2,500 BCE. People begin to settle in one place rather than move around.

55 BCE

In 55 BCE, the Roman emperor **Julius Caesar** invades Britain for the first time. He believes Britain is helping the French attack the Romans. He also wants to mine minerals such as tin, copper and lead.

793 CE

The **Vikings** first raid Britain in 793 CE. They attack a monastery on the island of Lindisfarne, off the north-east coast of England.

449 CE

The Romans leave Britain. Around 449 CE the **Angles and Saxons**, from mainland Europe, begin to settle in south-east Britain.

1066

William the Conqueror, from Normandy in France, invades southern Britain in 1066. He defeats Anglo-Saxon king Harold Godwinson to take the crown.

1215

The **Magna Carta** is signed by King John in 1215. It is one of the most important documents in British history. It guarantees rights for individuals, limits the monarchy's power and gives people access to the legal system.

1348

In 1348, the **plague** arrives in Britain. This disease goes on to kill tens of thousands of people.

1400

In 1400, the prince of Wales, Owain Glyn Dwr, leads his first **attack against England**. He is finally defeated in 1409.

1485

The **Tudor reign** begins after Henry VII defeats King Richard III at the Battle of Bosworth Field in 1485.

5 NOV 1605

On 5 November 1605, the **gunpowder plot** to kill King James I at Westminster Palace is discovered.

1908

London hosts the **Olympic Games** for the first time in 1908. It will go on to stage the Games again in 1948 and 2012.

1837

Queen Victoria takes the British throne in 1837. She rules until her death in 1901.

1 JAN 1801

On 1 January 1801, the **Act of Union** is signed. England, Scotland, Wales and Ireland are formally joined to create the UK (United Kingdom).

1666

1666 sees the **Great Fire of London** destroy around two-thirds of the city.

1914

Britain fights again against the Central Powers of Germany and Austria-Hungary in 1914, in a conflict known as the **First World War**.

1922

Ireland is divided in two in 1922, to establish Northern Ireland in the north and the **Republic of Ireland** in the south.

1936

In December 1936, King **Edward VIII** leaves the throne and his brother, George VI, becomes king.

2015

In September 2015, **Queen Elizabeth II** becomes the longest-reigning British monarch. She was crowned in 1952.

1989

In 1989, an Englishman called Sir Tim Berners-Lee invents the **World Wide Web**, which will change the world of communication forever.

1939

The **Second World War** begins in 1939 and lasts until 1945.

Iconic islands

From fish and chips and complaining about the weather to leprechauns and castles, there are lots of things – some real and some fake – that people associate with Britain and Ireland.

The Red Arrows are the aerobatics display team of the Royal Air Force (RAF). They perform in Britain and all over the world to millions of people each year.

Most Brits spend an average of **18** hours queueing per year.

44 per cent of British people think queuing is worse than doing the washing up!

The **Marmite** yeast paste was first made in 1902 in Staffordshire, England. Its distinctive taste has meant the word 'Marmite' is used to describe something people either love or hate.

The Queen has summer garden parties every year at Buckingham Palace, London or Holyrood Palace, Edinburgh. The **30,000 guests** get through …

27,000 cups of tea

20,000 sandwiches

20,000 slices of cake

Some of the most famous things that people connect to England, Ireland, Scotland and Wales don't even exist …

UNICORN

LEPRECHAUN

LOCH NESS
MONSTER

DRAGON

✦ Made up of nine red Hawk T1 jets ✦ Performed over 4,500 displays ✦ Based at RAF Scampton in Lincolnshire

✦ Formed in **1964** ✦ Watched by **1** BILLION people on TV as part of London **2012** Olympics opening ceremony.

Yeoman Warder is the official name of the 'Beefeater' guards at the Tower of London. Their origin goes back to the 14th century when they guarded the Tower, its prisoners and the Crown Jewels.

British people are well known for their love of drinking tea. It first became popular in wealthy families in the late 16th century, and when the tea tax was heavily reduced in **1784**, the working classes could suddenly afford a nice 'cuppa'.

The British drink **165** MILLION cups of tea a day, which is **60.2** BILLION cups a year!

Tea bags first appeared in the UK in the 1950s.

The Queen drinks Twinings' English Breakfast tea in the morning.

The iconic red British phone box first appeared on British streets in **1926**.

9

Monuments and sculptures

These structures, statues and sculptures are some of the most impressive – and strange – in Britain and Ireland. Some people love them and others hate them, but they have all made a big impact on the landscape.

Kissing the **Blarney Stone** is said to be give you the ability to talk in a humorous and witty way. The stone was set into a wall in Blarney Castle, in south-west Ireland, in the 1440s and millions of people are believed to have kissed it.

The Spinnaker Tower in Portsmouth is on the south coast of England. It's an observation tower, which can be seen 37 kilometres away and was built to look like a ship's sail.

Blackpool Tower is a tourist attraction in the English seaside town of Blackpool. It was finished in 1894 and was built as a replica of the Eiffel Tower in Paris, which is 324 metres tall.

The London Eye is a huge Ferris wheel on the banks of the River Thames in London. It gives passengers amazing views of the whole city.

The Spire of Dublin, in the Republic of Ireland, was completed in 2003, and is one of the most striking monuments in the city.

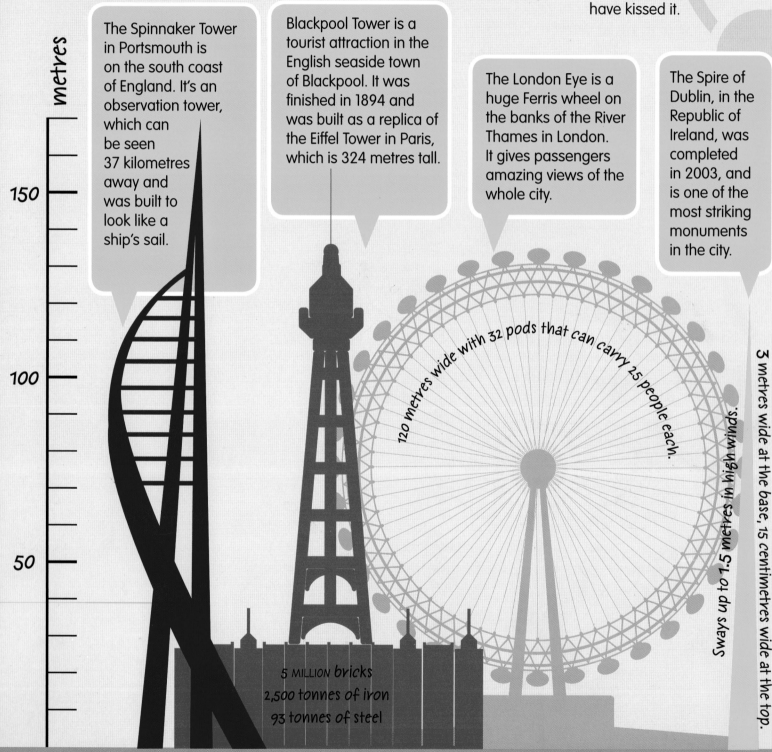

metres

150

100

50

120 metres wide with 32 pods that can carry 25 people each.

Sways up to 1.5 metres in high winds.

3 metres wide at the base, 15 centimetres wide at the top.

5 MILLION bricks
2,500 tonnes of iron
93 tonnes of steel

Spinnaker Tower	Blackpool Tower	London Eye	Spire of Dublin
170 m	158 m	135 m	120 m

Big Ben weighs **13,760** KILOGRAMS. It's the biggest bell in the Elizabeth Tower.

4.2 METRES is the length of the clock's minute hand.

A statue celebrating the first Duke of Wellington is often seen with a **traffic cone** on its head in the centre of Glasgow, Scotland.

Cone Head is the nickname the statue has been given.

Six **concrete cows** are the most well-known sculptures of the city of Milton Keynes in Buckinghamshire, England. They were made in 1978, and the three cows and three calves are about half the size of real-life cows.

The ancient Lligwy Burial Chamber, on the island of Anglesey off the coast of Wales, is 5,000 years old. It is formed of eight low stones which support a 25-tonne capstone across the top of them.

In **1908**, the bones of up to **30** people were found in the burial chamber.

Any chance you can move that stone off my head?

25 tonne

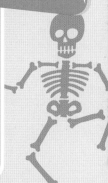

Big Ben is the nickname of the clock tower at the Palace of Westminster in central London. It was finished in 1859, and its official name is now the Elizabeth Tower.

Nelson's Column is a monument in London to Lord Nelson, who died at the Battle of Trafalgar in 1805.

£47,000 to build in the 1840s.

£420,000 to refurbish in 2006.

The Albert Memorial Clock is 43 metres tall, in the Northern Ireland capital, Belfast. Constructed in 1869, it used to lean 1.25 metres until restoration work corrected the tilt.

The *Angel of the North* is a steel sculpture, which was unveiled in 1998. It stands on a hill near Gateshead in north-east England.

It's wider than Nelson's Column is tall.

The biggest horses in Scotland are the 30-metre high *Kelpies* – two giant 300-tonne steel structures. The horse heads come up from the ground. Visitors to the attraction in Falkirk can even stand inside the sculptures.

A steel sculpture of a Welsh miner, called *Guardian*, stands at Abertillery in south Wales. It commemorates the 45 miners killed after a gas explosion in the Six Bells mine in 1960.

54-metre wingspan.

Big Ben	Nelson's Column	Albert Memorial Clock	Kelpies	Angel of the North	Guardian
96 m	51.6 m	43 m	30 m	20 m	20 m

A royal occasion

You can't think of British and Irish history without thinking of kings and queens. There are so many stories to tell and royals to explore across more than 1,000 years of history.

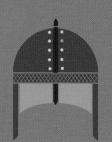

Anglo-Saxon and Viking kings of England, who battled each other, are known by some quite unusual names …

Alfred the Great (reigned 871–899)

Ethelred the Unready (978–1013 and 1014–1016)

Sweyn Forkbeard (1013–1014)

Edmund Ironside (1016)

Harald Harefoot (1035–1040)

Harthacnut (1040–1042)

HASTINGS

In 1066, King Harold of England's army fought Duke William of Normandy and his forces at the Battle of Hastings. King Harold lost and William became William I.

Lady Jane Grey only reigned as Queen of England for nine days in 1553. King Edward VI said Jane should become queen after his death, but a group of advisers declared Mary I the new queen.

700 · 800 · 900 · 1000 · 1100 · 1200 · 1300

Llywelyn ap Gruffydd was the last king of Wales before it was conquered by Edward I of England in around 1282.

A secret cave in Aberystwyth, west Wales, was once home to the **Crown Jewels**. The jewels were moved there from London during the Second World War to protect them.

The Crown Jewels are a collection of crowns, orbs, sceptres, swords and other treasures that kings and queens use at ceremonies. They are kept at the Tower of London and some experts value them at over £1 BILLION.

Henry VIII had SIX wives: Catherine of Aragon, Anne Boleyn, Jane Seymour, Anne of Cleves, Catherine Howard and Catherine Parr.

He had at least 11 children. Several of them died when they were young.

He became King of England aged 17, in 1509.

He was married to his first wife for 22 years, longer than his next five wives put together.

He was king for 37 years, between April 1509 and January 1547.

Henry weighed 170 kilograms towards the end of his life.

Some experts think 70,000 people could have been executed during Henry's reign.

Queen Elizabeth I (reigned 1558–1603) didn't like many of the portrait paintings of her because she thought they made her look ugly. At one point she ordered artists to just copy the one painting of herself that she liked.

Since the Kingdom of Great Britain was formed on 1 May 1707, there have been **twelve monarchs**. In 1801, the Kingdom of Ireland became part of Great Britain. In 1922, when Northern Ireland and the Irish Free State were created, it became the United Kingdom of Great Britain and Northern Ireland.

Queen Anne, 1707–1714
King George I, 1714–1727
King George II, 1727–1760
King George III, 1760–1820
King George IV, 1820–1830
King William IV, 1830–1837
Queen Victoria, 1837–1901
King Edward VII, 1901–1910
King George V, 1910–1936
King Edward VIII, 1936
King George VI, 1936–1952
Queen Elizabeth II, 1952–present day

1600

1700

1500

King James VI of Scotland also became King James I of England and Ireland in 1603, until his death in 1625.

Queen Victoria and her husband, Prince Albert, bought **Balmoral Castle** for £32,000 in 1852. That's the same as £4 million today.

1800

1400

1900

2000

The Queen has four official homes.

She also has two private residences.

Balmoral Castle, Aberdeenshire, Scotland

Holyrood Palace, Edinburgh, Scotland

Hillsborough Castle, County Down, Northern Ireland

As of 9 September 2015, Queen Elizabeth II had reigned for **23,226 days**. She became Britain's longest-reigning Monarch, beating the record of her great-great grandmother Queen Victoria.

DAY 23,226

Sandringham House, Norfolk, England

RIP

The only monarch to be born and die at Buckingham Palace was Edward VII. He was born there in 1841 and died in 1910.

Windsor Castle, Windsor, England

Buckingham Palace, London, England

Come rain or shine

The British and Irish are famous for talking about the weather! These islands enjoys all sorts of weather, from the extreme cold and snow of the Highlands to the warm sunshine of Jersey and Guernsey in the Channel Islands.

COLDEST TEMPERATURES RECORDED:

–18.7°C
Northern Ireland
24 December 2010
Castlederg,
County Tyrone

–19.1°C
Republic of Ireland
16 January 1881
Markree Castle,
County Sligo

–23.3°C
Wales
21 January 1940
Rhayader, Powys

–26.1°C
England
10 January 1982
Newport,
Shropshire

–27.2°C
Scotland
30 December 1995
Altnaharra,
Highlands

228.5 KPH is the highest-ever wind gust speed in the UK. It was recorded on 13 February 1989, in Fraserburgh, Scotland.

The last ice sheets and glaciers covering Britain dispersed **14,000** years ago. Some remained in the Scottish Highlands until about **10,000** years ago.

The UK gets **23.7** days of snow or sleet per year on average.

The Cairngorms in Scotland is the snowiest place, with **76.2** days of snow.

Cornwall is the least likely to get snow, with **7.4** days on average.

WETTEST PLACE
Crib Goch in north Wales gets **4,635** mm of rain per year on average.

SUNNIEST PLACE
St Helier, Jersey, averages **1,917** hours of sunshine a year.

Snow showers in England on 2 June 1975 forced many cricket games to be stopped!

The UK has **29** offshore wind farms and produces more electricity from wind than any other country in the world.

The **Great Storm** struck the UK on 15 and 16 October 1987. Extremely bad weather from the Bay of Biscay caused a surprising amount of damage.

Wind gusts up to **160** KPH.

About **15** MILLION trees blown down.

18 PEOPLE died in England.

The Met Office is the UK's national weather service. It has over **200** automatic weather stations around Britain, which record data such as air temperature, rainfall, wind speed, humidity and cloud height.

Between 1607–1814 there were seven Frost Fairs on the frozen River Thames in London. The fairs included ice skating, fruit selling, barbers, pubs and music.

DRIEST PLACE
St Osyth in Essex gets only **513** mm of rain per year on average.

WETTEST 24 HOURS RECORDED:

Republic of Ireland: **243.5 mm** of rain – 18 September 1993, Cloone Lake, County Kerry

England: **279 mm** of rain – 18 July 1955, Martinstown, Dorset

Scotland: **238 mm** of rain, 17 January 1974 – Sloy Main Adit, Argyll and Bute

Wales: **211 mm** of rain, 11 November 1929 – Lluest Wen Reservoir, Mid Glamorgan

The **mackintosh raincoat** is named after Scottish inventor Charles Rennie Macintosh, who developed waterproof fabrics in the 18th century.

The North British Rubber Company made its first **waterproof rubber boots** in 1856. The Duke of Wellington wore knee-high leather boots so rubber boots were soon known as '**wellies**'.

HOTTEST TEMPERATURES RECORDED:

38.5°C
England
10 August 2003
Faversham, Kent

35.2°C
Wales
2 August 1990
Hawarden Bridge, Flintshire

33.3°C
Republic of Ireland
26 June 1887
Kilkenny, County Kilkenny

32.9°C
Scotland
9 August 2003
Greycrook, Borders

30.8°C
Northern Ireland
30 June 1976
Knockarevan, County Fermanagh

Crumbling castles

There are hundreds of castles to explore across Britain and Ireland, from huge buildings where people still live to tiny ruins on remote islands. Some are nearly 1,000 years old and each has its own tale to tell.

Windsor Castle in Berkshire, England is Europe's oldest and largest continually inhabited castle. Building began around 1070 and **40 monarchs** have lived there.

Windsor Castle's grounds cover an area the same as nine football pitches.

St George's Hall is the castle's biggest room and is **55.5** metres long.

1.5 MILLION gallons of water were needed to put out the Great Fire at Windsor Castle in **1992**. That's enough to fill two Olympic swimming pools.

The clocks in the castle's Great Kitchen are set **5** minutes fast, so that food is never served late to the Queen!

Edinburgh Castle, in Scotland, dates from the 12th century and was a royal residence until 1603. It was involved in many conflicts and thought to have had **26 attacks**, making it the most besieged castle in Britain or Ireland.

1.4 MILLION people visit Edinburgh Castle every year.

King James I of Scotland was born at the castle in **1566**, and became King James VI of England and Ireland in **1603**.

Edinburgh Castle sits on Castle Rock, which was formed from volcanic magma about **350** million years ago.

Alnwick Castle in Northumberland was used to film scenes in the first two Harry Potter films.

In **1672**, a bolt of lightning destroyed the keep tower of Castle Cornet on the island of Guernsey, killing several people.

In 1215, King John of England attacked **Rochester Castle** in Kent. He used the fat from **40 pigs** to burn down its main tower, which helped him capture the castle.

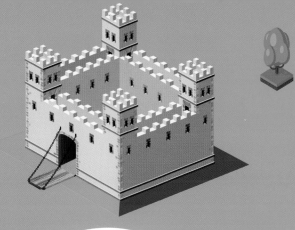

A **round table** hangs on a wall of the Great Hall at Winchester Castle, England. The table dates from about 1290 and is 5.5 metres wide and weighs 1,200 kg – the same weight as about three adult horses.

King John's Christmas feast at Winchester Castle in 1206, included:

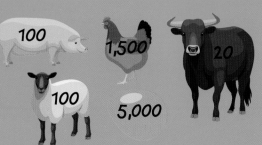

100
1,500
20
100
5,000

Bridgnorth Castle in Shropshire, England has a tower that tilts at **15 degrees** – that's four times more than the lean of the Leaning Tower of Pisa in Italy.

15°

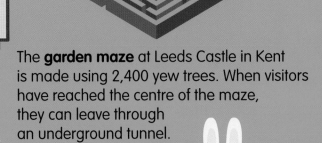

The **garden maze** at Leeds Castle in Kent is made using 2,400 yew trees. When visitors have reached the centre of the maze, they can leave through an underground tunnel.

Standing 450 metres above sea level, the remains of the Castell Dinas Brân fort in south Wales are the **highest castle** buildings in Britain and Ireland.

> Delivery! Only 999 more to come.

In 1935, Loch Doon Castle in Scotland was moved from an island and **rebuilt** on the mainland to save it from rising water levels. This meant thousands of stones being taken down and moved, one by one.

The remains of Dunluce Castle sit on the cliffs of County Antrim in Northern Ireland. In 1639, the owners were waiting for dinner one evening when the kitchen suddenly crumbled and **fell into the sea**.

> Anyone for fish?

The Countess of Dunbar defended Dunbar Castle in East Lothian, Scotland for **five months** with just a handful of guards. A bigger English army attacked in January 1338, but finally gave up on 10 June.

600 WELSH CASTLES

There are over **600 castles**, including castle ruins, in Wales. The largest is Caerphilly Castle in south Wales.

A walk in the countryside

Take a walk in the magnificent British or Irish countryside and you'll discover wildlife, animals and plants. The landscape can change drastically too, from the flat farms of eastern England to the mountain ranges of Scotland and Wales.

The largest living oak tree in Britain and Ireland is said to be the Bowthorpe Oak in Manthorpe, Lincolnshire, in east England.

- Estimated to be **1,000** years old
- **12.3** metres around the trunk
- **39** people once fitted inside its hollowed-out trunk.

The amount of **crops** grown in the UK each year depends on what the weather has been like. Wheat is grown the most, which is then used in foods, such as cereal and bread.

Wheat, **16** MILLION tonnes (per year)

Barley, **7** MILLION tonnes

Oilseed rape **2.5** MILLION tonnes

811 m

The highest hill in the Black Mountains is the Waun Fach, at 811 metres.

The Black Mountains are a range of hills in south-west Wales, and stretching into Herefordshire in England, that are mostly made of red sandstone rocks.

Sir Isaac Newton, the English scientist, watched apples fall from a tree at Woolsthorpe Manor farmhouse in Lincolnshire. He wondered why apples always fell straight down and later wrote about the idea of gravity.

The **Westbury White Horse** is a large, famous horse carved into the chalk grasslands on a hill near Westbury in Wiltshire, south-west England.

55 metres

52 metres

There is a **7.3**-metre stalactite in Doolin Cave on the west coast of Ireland. A stalactite is an icicle-like formation that hangs from a cave's ceiling.

The longest cave system in Britain and Ireland is called the Three Counties. It's found in the Yorkshire Dales in northern England. It is **89** kilometres long.

The depth of Ogof Ffynnon Ddu cave in south Wales is **307** metres. It is the deepest cave in Britain and Ireland.

A **white-tailed eagle** can grow a wingspan of up to 2.45 metres. It is the biggest bird of prey in Britain and Ireland. It is only found in north-west Scotland and there are around 40 breeding pairs left.

58 years old is the average age of a farmer in Britain and Ireland.

67 per cent is the amount of land used for agriculture across Britain and Ireland, which means the production of crops and breeding animals for food.

67%

Some endangered countryside species include:

- small tortoiseshell butterfly
- turtle dove
- Cosnard's net-winged beetle
- wart-biter cricket
- natterjack toad.

There are 2.5 million North American **grey squirrels** in the UK and only 140,000 red squirrels.

Red squirrels can mostly be found in Scotland, northern England and all across Northern Ireland.

An estimated 100,000 people climb Ben Nevis every year.

1,346 m

Ben Nevis, in the western Scottish Highlands, is the highest mountain in Britain and Ireland at 1,346 metres above sea level.

360,000 people climb Snowdon every year.

1,085 m

Snowdon is the highest mountain in Wales at 1,085 metres.

The largest forest in Scotland is Galloway Forest Park, at **776** square kilometres.

Clocaenog Forest is the largest forest in Wales, measuring **100** square kilometres.

West Fermanagh Upland is the biggest forest in Northern Ireland at **85** square kilometres.

The **hedgehog** is one of the most iconic creatures connected to the British countryside.

There are an estimated **1** million hedgehogs in the UK. In **1950**, there were about **36** million.

There are roughly 750,000 kilometres of hedgerows throughout Britain and Ireland. That's long enough to stretch from the Earth to the Moon, and back again!

School time

Ancient Romans set up schools in Britain about 2,000 years ago, but it wasn't until the late 19th century that all children had access to a free and regular education. All children between the ages of five and 18 must stay in education or training. Many choose to attend college or university.

OXFORD

Year founded	1096 approx
Number of students (2015)	22,602
Number of staff	12,500
British prime ministers	27
Nobel Prize winners	26
Overseas undergraduates	19%

Famous Oxford graduates include Sir Tim Berners-Lee, Hugh Grant and Baroness Margaret Thatcher.

CAMBRIDGE

Year founded	1209
Number of students (2015)	18,271
Number of staff	9,000
British prime ministers	14
Nobel Prize winners	92
Overseas undergraduates	11%

Famous Cambridge graduates include Sir Isaac Newton, Charles Darwin, Stephen Fry and Lily Cole.

The University Boat Race is an annual rowing race on the **River Thames**, in London, between Cambridge and Oxford. It began in 1829 and as of 2016, Cambridge has won **82** races to Oxford's **79**.

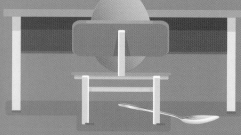

The first record of the **egg and spoon race** comes from 1890. It became a popular event at school sports days in 19th-century Britain.

Pendle College in Lancashire has a scary logo – the silhouette of a witch on a broomstick. The college is named after the infamous 17th-century **Pendle Witches**.

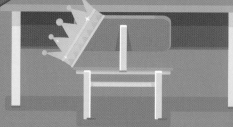

The King's School in Canterbury is often described as Britain and Ireland's **oldest school**. It is thought to have been founded about 597 CE.

Victorian schools in the 1800s were very different to the modern classrooms and teaching we know today:

- some inner-city schools had more than 70 children in a class
- Victorian school lessons could go on until 5 pm
- it became the law for all children to attend school in 1880
- the school leaving age was raised to 12 years old in 1899
- children usually wrote on small slates with chalk.

Educated animals

The University of York is famous for there being lots of ducks on its campus – it even has a **Duck of the Day** website, which pictures a new duck every day!

In 1996, scientists from the University of Edinburgh created the world's first cloned mammal. They created Dolly the sheep, who lived until she was six years old.

The poet **Lord Byron** kept a tame bear at Cambridge University in the 18th century.

Children at West Rise Junior school near Eastbourne, England, enjoy some unusual lessons within the school's **120 ACRES** of marshland:

- clay pigeon shooting
- archery
- fly fishing
- bee-keeping
- looking after water buffalo.

Eton College in Berkshire is a private boys' boarding school. It was formed by King Henry VI in 1440 to provide free education to 70 poor children and is now the most famous school in England.

Coventry University campus has a patch of grass with **old gravestones** on it. The university was built where a church once stood and the graves were not allowed to be removed.

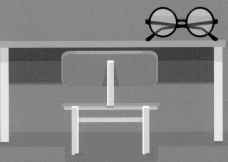

Harry Potter author J.K. Rowling took inspiration for **Hogwarts School** from the towering 17th-century George Heriot's School in Edinburgh.

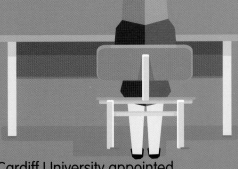

Cardiff University appointed a professor called Millicent McKenzie in 1904. She was the first **female professor** in the UK.

Fearsome fighting

The First and Second World Wars had a huge impact on British and Irish society over the last 100 years. But well before these battles, the English, Welsh, Scots and Irish were involved in wars and fighting that shaped everyday lives too.

The Battle of Hastings, which happened on **14 October 1066** between the English and Normans, is thought to have lasted just eight hours. It began at 9 a.m. and finished about 5 p.m.

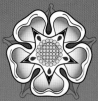

White Rose of York

The **Wars of the Roses** were a long series of wars fought over the English throne between the 1450s and 1480s. It involved a number of battles between the two sides – the House of York and the House of Lancaster.

Red Rose of Lancaster

Henry Tudor, from the House of Lancaster, killed Richard III of the House of York at the Battle of Bosworth Field in 1485. He became King Henry VII.

Tudor Rose

The Nine Years' War (1594–1603) was fought in Ireland between an Irish army, led by the Earl of Tyrone, and the English.

KINGS KILLED IN BATTLE

Macbeth of Scotland
Battle of Lumphanan, 1057
Aberdeenshire, Scotland.

Richard III of England
Battle of Bosworth Field, 1485
Leicestershire, England.

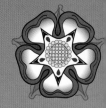

James IV of Scotland
Battle of Flodden, 1513
Northumberland, England.

The Hundred Years' War (1337–1453) took place throughout France, Spain, England and Belgium between the French and English. It actually lasted for **116** years!

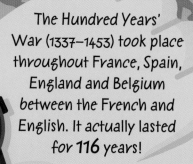

The last **invasion** on Britain's mainland was in 1797 in Fishguard, on the south-west coast of Wales. Around 1,500 French troops landed there, but a small group were captured by a heroic local woman called Jemima Nicholas.

The **Spitfire** was a fighter plane used by the RAF during the Second World War (1939–1945). It played a key role in the Battle of Britain air combats against German planes in 1940.

Great Britain fought in the **First World War** against the Central Powers of Germany and Austria-Hungary between 1914 and 1918.

By October **1914**, millions had joined the army to help the war effort.

In May **1915**, German Zeppelin airships began bombing London.

By the end of **1917**, the war was costing Britain £6 million a day.

The fighting came to an end after Germany signed the Armistice on 11 November **1918**.

Pigeons were used in the First World War and Second World War to carry secret messages. The most successful and bravest pigeons could even win the Dickin Medal for their courage.

KEEP CALM AND CARRY ON

This poster was created in **1939**, with the hope of keeping people calm before the possible outbreak of the Second World War.

DEFENCE OF THE REALM ACT

The Defence of the Realm Act was enacted by the British government in August 1939 to help the war effort. Some of its stranger laws included:

- no buying binoculars
- no feeding bread to wild animals
- no flying of kites.

The Battle of Culloden, in the Scottish Highlands, was fought in 1746. It was the last 'pitched battle' on British land, which means a place and a **start time** for the fighting was agreed between the two sides. King George II's troops beat Bonnie Prince Charlie's army at the battle.

Tasty treats

From cheese to crisps, sandwiches to strawberries and pasties to potatoes, Britain and Ireland have stacks of weird and wonderful food that they make, eat and sell.

CORNWALL

The pasty was a popular food in **Cornwall**, south-west England, by the 18th century. Cornish miners took pasties underground and ate them during the day.

Over 120 MILLION Cornish pasties are made each year.

Cornish pasty production generates £300 MILLION for Cornwall.

A 4-kilogram Double Gloucester cheese reaches more than **110 kph** when it is rolled down Cooper's Hill in Gloucestershire's annual cheese-rolling event.

During the two-week tournament, hungry spectators at the Wimbledon Tennis Championships, in south London, will get through ...

110,000 sandwiches
140,000 portions of strawberries
86,000 ice-cream portions
30,000 pizzas

FINISH

1837 is the year Worcestershire Sauce was first bottled and sold in Worcester, England. It's now exported to over **130** countries.

Scottish haggis is a dish traditionally eaten on **Burns Night** (25 January) to celebrate the Scottish poet Robert Burns. The main ingredients of haggis are sheep's heart, liver and lungs, plus onion, oats and spices.

CRISPS

About **7 MILLION** bags of crisps are made every day at the Walkers Crisps factories in Leicestershire, England.

The leek is one of the national symbols of **Wales**. Traditionally soldiers in Welsh regiments eat a raw leek on St David's Day (1 March).

The world's oldest Oyster festival takes place in Galway in the Republic of Ireland. It attracts **22,000** people each year.

LINCOLNSHIRE

The English county of Lincolnshire produces over **20 per cent** of all foodstuffs grown in the UK.

Lincolnshire, and the Fens region of Cambridgeshire and Norfolk, grow enough wheat to make **250** MILLION loaves of bread a year.

Farms in the Fens grow **1.5** MILLION tonnes of potatoes each year.

Britain's favourite biscuits:

1. Chocolate digestive
2. Chocolate Hobnob
3. Custard cream
4. Shortbread
5. Jaffa Cake
6. Cookie
7. Digestive
8. Ginger nut
9. Chocolate bourbon
10. Chocolate finger

Why are British sausages called bangers? The name comes from sausages made during the First World War, which had lots of water in them and often popped and banged when being cooked.

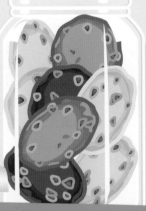

A hamburger:

10p **5p**

A cheeseburger:

20p **1p**

A value meal:

20p **20p**

5p **2p** **1p**

Britain's first McDonald's restaurant opened in Woolwich, south-east London, in 1974. The prices were a lot cheaper then ...

180,000 tonnes of salmon are caught in Scottish waters every year and sold for food.

Over **1 MILLION** Stilton cheeses are made each year. By law, Stilton cheese can only be made in the English counties of **Derbyshire**, **Leicestershire** and **Nottinghamshire**.

Britain's first fish fingers were produced by Birds Eye in Great Yarmouth, Norfolk, in 1955. More than **1** MILLION are now eaten every day in Great Britain.

FISH FINGERS

Amazing animals

There are millions of people living and working in Britain and Ireland, but there are even more animals! From birds to bears and pandas to ponies, read on to find out about the creatures on these shores.

Victoria Park, in Cardiff, Wales, was home to a **seal** in the 20th century. Billy the seal lived in a pond from 1915 to 1939, and there's now a sculpture in the park to remember him.

London Zoo is the world's **oldest scientific zoo** and was opened to the public in 1847.

Around **17 million** birds use these islands for migration. This means they arrive here to feed, breed or escape from cold weather in other parts of the world.

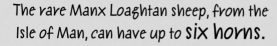

32.8 million sheep are estimated to be in Great Britain.

Jumbo the elephant arrived in **1865**.

Winnie the bear arrived in **1914**.

Guy the gorilla arrived on Guy Fawkes night, **1947**.

1900

2000

The rare Manx Loaghtan sheep, from the Isle of Man, can have up to **six horns**.

500,000 sheep are sold each year at the Welshpool sheep market in central Wales.

90 sheep breeds and cross-breeds are found in the UK. No other country has this many.

ZOO

THE ZOO

Daisy the Elephant was shipped to Belfast dock in Northern Ireland in the **1940s**. She walked 9.5 kilometres to Belfast Zoo.

Female panda, Tian Tian, and male panda, Yang Guang, arrived at Edinburgh Zoo, Scotland, in **2011**. It is the only British or Irish zoo with giant pandas.

English author A.A. Milne saw Winnie the bear at London Zoo and later wrote the famous children's books about Winnie-the-Pooh.

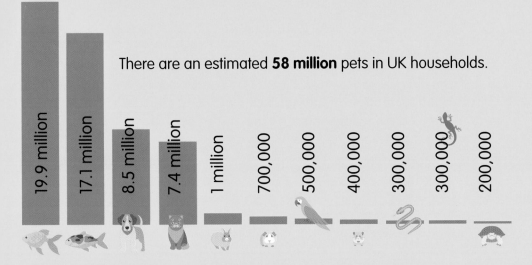

There are an estimated **58 million** pets in UK households.

19.9 million	17.1 million	8.5 million	7.4 million	1 million	700,000	500,000	400,000	300,000	300,000	200,000

The 100-metre high **Bass Rock**, off the east coast of Scotland, is home to the largest colony of northern gannet birds. More than 150,000 nest there.

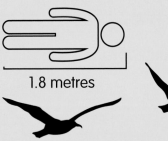

1.8 metres

King Henry III was given a white bear, thought to be a **polar bear**, by the king of Norway in 1252. The bear was kept at the Tower of London and often went swimming in the River Thames, attached to a long leash.

The gannets are the **largest sea bird** in Britain and Ireland, with a wingspan of more than 1.8 metres.

They dive into the water at speeds of up to **95 kph**.

The UK has approximately **1.89 million dairy cows**! The famous black and white Holstein-Friesian breed is the most popular and makes up 90 per cent of the cows. Other breeds include Ayrshire, Jersey and Guernsey cows.

10%

90%

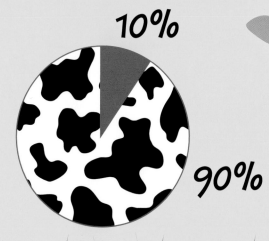

British dairy farmers produce around **11 billion litres** of milk every year. A whopping **6,914 million litres** of milk is sold for drinking.

An estimated **1,500 wild goats** roam the Scottish Highlands.

A **gwyniad** is a fish that only lives in Bala Lake in north-west Wales. It was left behind at the end of the last ice age.

There are an estimated **3,000 ponies** living wild in the New Forest in Hampshire in the south of England.

Around **1,000 wild boar** live in the Forest of Dean in Gloucestershire, England – the largest population in the UK.

Game on!

Britain and Ireland are home to a huge variety of sports with millions of people taking part or watching every week. Whether it's football, rugby, athletics, cycling, golf or tennis there is always an exciting sporting event going on.

Wembley football stadium, in north-west London, is the biggest sporting venue in Britain and Ireland. It holds 90,000 fans, has 2,618 toilets, 98 kitchens and 54 kilometres of seating.

England won the World Cup, the world's biggest football competition, at the original Wembley stadium in **1966**.

Northern Ireland's most famous sportsman was a footballer called **George Best**, who was born in Belfast in 1946. He first played for Manchester United in England aged 17 and scored 179 goals in 470 games for the club.

The world's first official game of football, with rules similar to those used now, took place in **1848** in a Cambridge park in England.

The **Premier League** is the top level of football in England and Wales.

PREMIER LEAGUE WINNERS 1992–2016	
Manchester United	13
Chelsea	4
Arsenal	3
Manchester City	2
Leicester City	1
Blackburn Rovers	1

Oliver Cromwell was Lord Protector of the Commonwealth of England, Scotland and Ireland. He wasn't a sports fan, though, and banned several sports.

The Chester Racecourse, in north-west England, is Britain's oldest sporting venue still in continual use. The first horse race was in 1539, when Henry VIII was king.

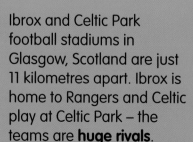

MORE FOOTBALL
11 kilometres

Ibrox and Celtic Park football stadiums in Glasgow, Scotland are just 11 kilometres apart. Ibrox is home to Rangers and Celtic play at Celtic Park – the teams are **huge rivals**.

Top UK horse races:

- Cheltenham Festival, Cheltenham
- The Grand National, Liverpool
- Guineas Meeting, Newmarket
- Royal Ascot, Berkshire
- Welsh Grand National, Chepstow.

London is the only city to have hosted the **Olympic Games** three times. It staged the world's greatest sporting competition in 1908, 1948 and 2012.

2000

1996

1988

1984

1980

English rower Sir Steve Redgrave is the only sportsperson to win gold medals in endurance sport at five consecutive Olympic Games.

The **Six Nations** is an annual rugby tournament. The national teams of England, Scotland, Wales, Ireland, France and Italy compete. It began in 1883 with England, Scotland, Wales and Ireland – France joined in 1910 and Italy in 2000.

Outright wins from 1883–2016:

ENGLAND	WALES	FRANCE	SCOTLAND	IRELAND UTD	ITALY

27	26	17	15	13	0

3,000 years That's how old the Irish field sport of hurling is thought to be. Two teams of 15 players use a wooden stick, called a hurley, to hit a small ball between two goal posts or over the other team's cross-bar.

The annual tennis Championships at **Wimbledon**, in south-west London, are the most prestigious in the world.

Wimbledon began in **1877**, making it the world's oldest tennis tournament.

More than **54,250** tennis balls are used during the two-week tournament.

236 kph is the fastest serve recorded at Wimbledon, by Australian player Sam Groth.

The **Old Course** at St Andrews, on the east coast of Scotland, is believed to be the oldest golf course in the world, dating back over 450 years.

There are over 550 golf courses in Scotland.

In **1889**, Scottish golfers William Bloxsom and Arthur Douglas invented the first golf tee, for resting the ball on.

The **Tour of Britain** is an annual men's road cycle race for professional riders around Scotland, Wales and England.

In 2016, the total race length was 1294.2 kilometres.

There were eight stages over eight days that included places such as Glasgow in Scotland, Carlisle in England and Denbigh in Wales.

A land of culture

Britain and Ireland are bursting with culture, art, music, festivals and theatre. From classical music composers and talented writers to street artists and children's entertainers, there's something for everyone …

Britain's most iconic artist of the 21st century is a man who no one knows. **Banksy** is a street artist who sprays and paints art on walls, buildings and public places. His work has strong political and social meaning, and his identity is a secret.

The Republic of Ireland has won the Eurovision Song Contest a record SEVEN times. It's an annual song competition where a singer or a group represent their country, with most European countries taking part.

For auld lang syne, my dear, For auld lang syne
We'll take a cup of kindness yet, For auld lang syne

JANUARY 1

'Auld Lang Syne' is a Scottish poem written by Robert Burns. The poem's chorus is traditionally sung at midnight on New Year's Eve.

Hogmanay is the word Scottish people use for the last day of the year and New Year's Eve celebrations.

The **Royal Albert Hall** is a world famous concert hall in London, which was opened by **Queen Victoria** in 1871. The hall is named after Victoria's husband, **Prince Albert**.

Originally the building contained about **6** MILLION bricks.
The hall is the height of **10** DOUBLE–DECKER BUSES piled on top of each other, with a London taxi sitting on the top.
The hall's organ has **9,999** PIPES.

Famous British classical composers:
- George Frideric Handel (1685-1759)
- Sir Edward William Elgar (1857-1934)
- Gustav Holst (1874-1934)
- Benjamin Britten (1913-1976)

The name is Bond … James Bond is a popular fictional British spy created by English author Ian Fleming (1908–1964). Fleming wrote 14 James Bond books, and 24 films have been released.

Pantomime theatre has its roots in Italy and France, but by the Victorian era it had become a popular Christmas theatre attraction in Britain.

Pantomime villains

Wicked stepmother – Cinderella

The giant – Jack and the Beanstalk

The wicked witch – The Wizard of Oz

It's behind you! Oh, no, it isn't!

The traditional seaside children's puppet show, PUNCH AND JUDY, was first performed in Britain in **1662**.

In the popular Punch and Judy story, a hungry crocodile steals Punch's raw sausages.

British pop music has been popular since the late 1950s. From rock 'n' roll to punk and Britpop, there has always been a certain sound to British music.

Pobol y Cwm is a Welsh-language BBC television soap opera that was first shown in 1974. It's the oldest TV soap opera made by the BBC.

Estimated sales

The Beatles		600 million
Elton John		350 million
Led Zeppelin		300 million
Queen		300 million

1974   1985   2016

In **2014**, one in every seven albums sold globally was recorded by a British artist, including One Direction, Ed Sheeran and Coldplay.

Glastonbury festival takes place every year at Worthy Farm in Somerset. It's the most popular music and performing arts festival in the world!

200,000 festival-goers attend.

34,000 staff and volunteers.

5,000 toilets on site.

2,000 pairs of wellies are left behind.

900 acres of land are used.

Cruise around the coast

At more than 17,500 kilometres Britain and Ireland have more coastline than countries such as India, Brazil or South Africa. These islands are home to beaches, cliffs, wildlife, millions of people … and quite a few deckchairs.

Murlough Nature Reserve, on the coast of County Down in Northern Ireland, is a 6,000-year-old sand dune system. In 1967, it became Ireland's first nature reserve.

The Normans created a **rabbit warren** in the dunes so they could use the animals for food.

Approximately **3 million** people live on the coast in the UK.

The Republic of Ireland's coastline is about **1,450 kilometres** long.

Nowhere in the UK is more than **113 km** from the coast.

The town of Cromer, on the north Norfolk coast, is famous for the Cromer crab. The World Pier **Crabbing Championships** are held every year on Cromer Pier.

There are **130** recorded shipwrecks around the rocks at Land's End.

Mainland Great Britain's coast is **17,820** KILOMETRES long.

The first Longships Lighthouse was built in **1795** to warn ships and boats away from the rocks.

Land's End in Cornwall, England, is the most westerly point in England.

Southend Pier: **2,158** metres long

Southport Pier: **1,112** metres long

Walton-on-the-Naze Pier: **793** metres long

Ryde Pier: **660** metres long

ESSEX

The Essex coastline is more than **560** kilometres long, the longest in England.

Southend Pier in Essex is the longest pier in the world. It's as long as **196** double-decker buses.

There are **35** islands along the Essex coast. Most are uninhabited by humans.

7 ×

The **Royal National Lifeboat Institution** (RNLI) is a charity that saves lives in the seas around the coast of the UK, Ireland, the Channel Islands and the Isle of Man.

- established in **1824**
- **324** lifeboats
- **236** lifeboat stations
- saved **144,000** lives since 1824
- over **200** beaches patrolled by RNLI lifeguards.

The **Giant's Causeway**, on the coast of County Antrim in Northern Ireland, is an area of rock caused by a volcanic eruption millions of years ago. It has about 40,000 columns and is up to 12 metres high. It's called the Giant's Causeway because, in Irish legend, a giant called Finn MacCool built the causeway so he could reach Scotland to fight another giant.

No vacancies
Top **10** Most Popular English Seaside Resorts
1. Blackpool
2. Brighton
3. Whitby
4. Bournemouth
5. Scarborough
6. Newquay
7. Torquay
8. St Ives
9. Skegness
10. Great Yarmouth

Victorian seaside activities:
- donkey rides on the beach
- building sandcastles
- paddling in the sea
- having a picnic
- walking on the pier.

Worms Head is a 1.6-milometre long stretch of rock sticking out from the coast at Rhossili in south Wales. At low tide you can walk over a limestone arch called **Devil's Bridge**.

The **Jurassic Coast** stretches more than 150 kilometres from east Devon to east Dorset on the south coast of England. Its rocks and cliffs were formed as much as 185 million years ago.

The sea cliffs at Croaghaun, County Mayo, in the Republic of Ireland are **688 metres** high.

Lulworth Cove in Dorset is a natural, horseshoe-shaped cove that was formed by the sea about **10,000** years ago.

200,000 people walk between Lulworth Cove and Durdle Door each year.

Durdle Door is a natural limestone arch on the Jurassic Coast. It was formed MILLIONS of years ago.

Brighton has more than **3,000** deckchairs available for hire.

The highest sea cliff in England is called Great Hangman. It is found on the Devon coast and is **244 metres** high.

Interesting inventions

From machines, medicines, technology, vehicles, toys and fashion, Britain and Ireland have launched some of the most important creations of the last 250 years …

1590s
Sir John Harrington invented the first **flush toilet**. In America, 'going to the John' is a common term for going to the toilet.

1798
Edward Jenner created the world's first vaccine, against the **smallpox disease**.

1801
Richard Trevithick powered a piston using high-pressure steam, which lead to the **steam engine**.

1810
Peter Durand came up with the idea of using a **tin can** to preserve food.

The **Sinclair C5** single-seater electric vehicle was built by Sir Clive Sinclair in 1985 in Merthyr Tydfil, Wales. It quickly became one of the worst British inventions of the decade.

- C5 had a top speed of just **24** kph
- battery only lasted for **32** kilometres
- It cost **£399**
- the C5 struggled to get up big hills
- users got wet when it rained.

The British **Mini** car was launched in 1959, at a time when petrol was very expensive and small cars were seen as the future of motoring. It was just 3 metres long, had a small 850 cc engine and could reach just 119 kph.

Sir Tim Berners-Lee is an English computer scientist whose work led to the creation of the **World Wide Web** in 1989. He created the first web browser and the world's first website address was …

http://info.cern.ch

1831
Michael Faraday discovered electromagnetic induction – **electricity** – in simple terms.

1840
Sir Rowland Hill reformed the postal system and introduced the **postage stamp**.

1853
Alexander Wood invented the hypodermic **syringe needle**.

Freddie Francis is the man who invented Scalextric slot racing car. Freddie's company made mini toy cars in the 1940s and '50s, but in 1957 he released the first Scalextric electric slot car system.

In 1960, shoemaker Bill Griggs made the first pair of **Dr. Martens** boots in the UK. With a soft AirWair sole and distinctive yellow stitching, the famous black boots became an icon of British fashion loved by workmen, rock stars and musicians.

Each boot takes around 1.5 hours to create.

The sole of a Dr. Martens boot is made of around 20,000 tiny PVC beads that are melted down.

Concorde aircraft flew commercial flights for the first time in 1969.

Concorde was designed and built by the British Aircraft Corporation and the French-run Aerospatiale. It was an iconic plane that stopped flying in 2003.

Concorde could fly at 2,179 kph. A Boeing 757 reaches 1,580 kph.

It could fly between London and New York in under **three** hours. Normal flights take about **six** hours and 45 minutes.

Englishman, Frank Whittle, invented and developed the turbojet engine in the 1930s, a creation that led to jet-powered aircraft.

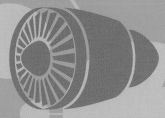

In 1978, British inventor James Dyson came up with the idea for a **bagless vacuum cleaner** that wouldn't lose suction. Five years later and after 5,127 prototypes, he invented the world's first bagless vacuum, which would become the Dyson.

Version

5,127

James Dyson is said to have a fortune of £3 BILLION.

English inventor and businessman Frank Hornby (1863–1936) is famous for creating three popular toys:

- Frank created the first metal Meccano construction sets in 1898 in Liverpool
- clockwork Hornby toy trains were released in 1920 and, in 1925, an electric Hornby toy
- in the 1930s, Frank Hornby's Meccano company created Dinky miniature die-cast toy cars.

1884
The **light switch** was invented by John Holmes.

1937
999 was introduced – the world's first **emergency telephone service**.

1966
James Goodfellow created PIN technology and the first **cash machine**.

1991
Trevor Bayliss invented the **wind-up radio**.

Weird and wonderful

It's time to discover some brilliant, baffling and bonkers facts and stories about the bizarre side of Britain and Ireland.

The **Republic of Ireland** is the world's only country to have a musical instrument as its national symbol: the harp.

A statue of a Skye Terrier dog is one of the most famous in Edinburgh, Scotland. It is called *Greyfriars Bobby* and commemorates a dog that lingered near the grave of its dead owner for 14 years.

007 is the name given to the fictional spy James Bond. Ian Fleming, the author of the James Bond books, used this number because it was the number of the bus that he used to catch.

250,000 turkeys had walked from Norfolk to London to be sold at markets by the mid-18th century. It was a distance of over 160 kilometres but it was the only practical, and cheap, way to move them.

Turkeys are thought to have first arrived in Britain in **1526**. William Strickland, from East Yorkshire, brought six of them to England from America.

LLANFAIRPWLLGWYNGYLLGOGERYCHWYRNDROBWYLLLLANTYSILIOGOGOGOCH

Llanfairpwllgwyngyllgogerychwyrndrobwyllllantysiliogogogoch is a small town on the island of Anglesey, off the north-west Welsh coast. It's the **longest place name** in Britain and Ireland. Locals call it Llanfair, which is much easier to say.

AE

The village of Ae, in the Dumfries and Galloway region of Scotland, has the **shortest name**.

Llanwrtyd Wells is a small town in Powys, west Wales. Since 1985 it has held the world **bog-snorkelling championship**, where competitors snorkel through 110 metres of messy bog water in the quickest time possible.

35 35 mph (56 kph) is the maximum speed limit in Guernsey, on the Channel Islands.

70 mph (113 kph) is the maximum speed limit in mainland Britain. **70**

The high stone walls of the **Hamilton Mausoleum**, which is a type of tomb, in South Lanarkshire, are said to have the longest echo in the world, lasting 15 seconds … seconds … seconds …

The Royal College of Physicians in Dublin, Republic of Ireland, has a **toothbrush** belonging to French Emperor Napoleon Bonaparte (1769–1821) on display. The toothbrush is around 200 years old!

Strange superstitions

Seeing **one magpie bird** by itself is reckoned to be an unlucky sign.

If the **six ravens** that live at the Tower of London should leave, the UK will fall and bad things will happen!

People often believe you'll get **seven years' bad luck** if you break a mirror.

It's often thought that **13** is an unlucky number. If the 13th day of any month is on a Friday, this is also an unlucky date.

The **Zip World Velocity** attraction, at Penrhyn Quarry in north Wales, is the highest zip wire in Europe.

It's **150** metres high and reaches speeds of **160** kph. **160**

The Queen celebrates **two birthdays** each year: her actual birthday on 21 April and her official birthday, usually the second Saturday in June.

When she's travelling overseas, the Queen does not need a passport.

The Queen has had 30 Corgi dogs since coming to the throne in 1952.

Home sweet home

Everyone likes a few home comforts, but in Britain and Ireland that could mean having 8 kilometres of corridors or being haunted by an ancient Egyptian mummy. Check out this collection of mighty mansions, tiny terraces and tall tower blocks.

No. 3

A circular structure found under a field near Scarborough, North Yorkshire, in 2010 is 10,500 years old. It's the **oldest remains** of a house in Britain and Ireland.

No. 2

Britain's **most northerly home** is on the isle of Unst, on the Shetland Isles to the north of Scotland. It is about 300 kilometres from Norway and 1,029 kilometres from London.

No. 1

The town of Tobermory, on the isle of Mull on Scotland's west coast, is home to some famous **brightly coloured houses**.

The BBC children's TV show *Balamory* was filmed in Tobermory.

No. 4

Wentworth Woodhouse in South Yorkshire, England, is the **largest private home** in Britain. It is 185 metres wide, which is 1.5 times the lengths of a full-size football pitch. It also has:

- 8 kilometres of corridors
- 350 rooms
- was bought for £8 MILLION in 2015.

No.8

Castletown House is a grand 18th century mansion in County Kildare, east Ireland. It's said to have inspired the building of the White House, home to the President of the United States.

No. 7

The **smallest house** in Britain is in Conwy, north Wales. It is:

- 1.82 metres wide
- 2.84 metres high
- 3.04 metres deep.

The terrace was last occupied in 1900. It is painted bright red with two small front windows.

No. 6

Queen Victoria died at **Osborne House** in 1901, on the Isle of Wight in the English Channel. Visitors to the house can see the room where she died – and even her bathtub.

No. 5

The **tallest residential building** in the Britain and Ireland is St George Wharf Tower in central London. It's 181 metres tall – nearly twice the height of Big Ben – and contains 214 apartments.

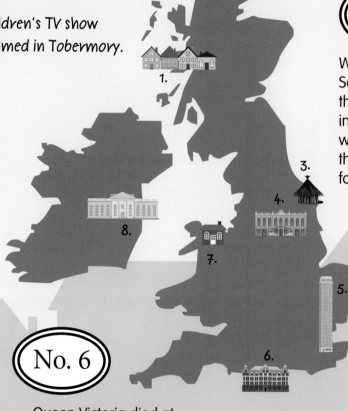

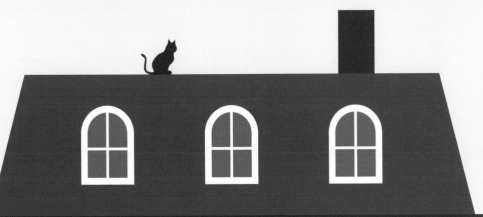

The first house in the world to be lit by electricity was a 19th-century country home called Cragside, in north-east England. Hydro-electricity was created using water from a nearby lake and powered the lights.

To put a roof over the heads of the 64 million people in Britain, lots of houses are needed.

- there are **25 MILLION** homes across Britain
- **141,000** new homes were finished in 2014
- **2 billion** bricks are made each year.

A 3,000-year-old Egyptian mummy is on display at Bodrhyddan Hall in Flintshire, north Wales. The house has been the residence of Lord Langley and his family for over **500** years.

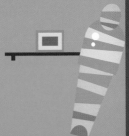

Grand mansion houses built from the middle ages onwards often had their **kitchen** in a separate building. If it caught fire, the main house was less likely to burn down.

In the early 1900s, the chocolate-makers Cadbury built 143 cottages for some of their workers to live in. The homes were built at Bourneville, just outside of Birmingham in England. **8,000** homes are now on the Bourneville estate.

UK's most popular house names

The Cottage

The Rose Cottage

Woodlands

The Old Post Office

The Stables

The Granary

Street talking

Streets, roads, lanes, alleys, passages, drives – the tarmac, concrete and stone pathways of Great Britain reveal all sorts of stories. Some are famous and some are infamous.

The **North West 200** is a street motorbike race between Portstewart, Coleraine and Portrush in Northern Ireland. Bikes reach speeds of over **320 kph** and 150,000 spectators line the streets to watch the action.

A is for Access Road, Liverpool

B is for Boghead Road, Dumbarton

C is for Crazy Lane, East Sussex

D is for Drip Road, Stirling

E is for Excellent Road, Hampshire

F is for Fair-A-Far Shot, Edinburgh

G is for Granny Lane, Leeds

H is for Hole in the Wall Road, Dublin

I is for Itchin Close, Southampton

J is for Joy Road, Gravesend

K is for Kissing Tree Lane, Stratford

L is for Little Britain Street, Dublin

M is for My Street, Salford

N is for No Name Street, Sandwich

O is for Off The Avenue, Nottinghamshire

P is for Porridge Pot Lane, Essex

PUDDING LANE is where the Great Fire of London began at a bakery on 2 September 1666.

13,200 HOUSES were destroyed.

87 CHURCHES burned down.

£10 MILLION of damage (same as £1.5 BILLION now).

Ebenezer Place in Wick, Scotland is **2.05 metres** long. It's the shortest street in the world!

Grovehill Junction in Beverly, East Yorkshire, has a whopping 42 sets of traffic lights to oversee where four roads come together.

HIGH STREET
There are around 3,000 streets in Britain called 'High Street'.

Buckingham Palace, the home of Queen Elizabeth II, does not have a street or road name in its address, but it has its own postcode: SW1A 1AA.

CORONATION STREET

The streets of Milton Keynes in Buckinghamshire are joined by **124 roundabouts.**

Coronation Street in **Manchester** is one of Britain's most famous streets … even though it's fake. It was built for the TV show, and is Britain's longest-running soap opera.

The **Royal Mile** is a famous group of streets in the Old Town of Edinburgh. It is just over 1.6 kilometres (1 mile) long and runs between Edinburgh Castle and Holyrood Palace.

10,000 people joined Britain's biggest street party on 12 June 2016. They sat at tables on The Mall, the long road leading up to Buckingham Palace, to celebrate the Queen's 90th birthday.

Q is for Quality Street, North Berwick

R is for Rotten Row, Southport

S is for Slippery Back, Tenby

The postcode **HD7 5UZ** in Huddersfield, covers seven streets. No other British postcode covers so many streets.

T is for There and Back Again Lane, Bristol

U is for Ugly Bridge Road, Warwick

V is for Van Road, Caerphilly

School

Lollipop men and women first appeared on Britain's streets in **1963**. Dressed in bright yellow coats, the sign they hold to stop traffic and allow school children to cross the road was soon nicknamed a lollipop sign.

Oxford Street is 2.4 km long – that's long enough to lay Big Ben flat along it 25 times.

W is for Whip-Ma-Whop-Ma-Gate, York

X is for ... no roads start with X!

Y is for Yet Mead Lane, Somerset

Z is for Zig Zag Road, Surrey

10 Downing Street has been the home of the British prime minister since 1735. The last private resident to live in the building was a man called Mr Chicken, who moved out in the early 1730s.

There are about **300** shops on the street.

500,000 people visit Oxford Street in central London every day. It is the busiest shopping street in Europe.

There are over **26,000** streets within a 9.65-kilometre (6-mile) radius of Charing Cross in London. Taxi drivers must study the streets for three years and pass a test before they can drive a London black cab.

Towering buildings

Exploring the different famous buildings all around Britain and Ireland is a great way to explore their history. Buildings on these pages were built from the 6th right up to the 21st century.

The BT Tower, which was first called the **Post Office Tower**, opened in London in 1964.

169 metres tall

£9 MILLION to build in 1960

13,000 tonnes

20 cm
Designed to sway 20 cm in winds up to 160 kph.

The Scottish Exhibition Centre, in Glasgow, is nicknamed the Armadillo because of the building's likeness to the animal.

'Dippy' the Diplodocus, a 32-metre long replica, was first displayed in the entrance hall at the Natural History Museum in London in 1979.

Westminster Abbey in London dates back to around 1060, although work on the current building began in 1245.

17 kings and queens have been buried there.

It's hosted **16** royal weddings, including the Duke and Duchess of Cambridge's ceremony in **2011**.

Liverpool has over 2,400 **listed buildings**. People who own a listed building must have permission from the local government before making changes to it.

15 metres

The Imperial Arch in Liverpool is the largest outside of Asia.

69 metres

The 6th-century chapel at Rhos-on-Sea in north Wales is 4 metres long and 3.3 metres wide. It is said to be the smallest church in Britain and Ireland with room for just six worshippers.

Coventry Cathedral in central England is a very distinctive building. It's made from the remains of a 14th century cathedral, which was bombed in the Second World War, and a modern 1950s building.

The lighthouse at La Corbiere in south-west Jersey is the most southerly lighthouse in the Britain and Ireland.

Stormont, the Northern Ireland Assembly, is **365 feet** (111 metres) wide. Feet is an old type of measurement – a 'foot' is 30 centimetres long. It is 365 feet to represent 365 days in year. There are also six floors for the six counties of Northern Ireland.

The Senedd building in Cardiff is home to the **National Assembly of Wales**. It opened in 2006, and in 2008, a Welsh law was passed for the first time since the 10th century.

The Skerryvore Lighthouse on the west coast of Scotland is the **tallest lighthouse** in Britain, with 151 steps to the top.

47.5 metres

1807 is the year that work began to build the Bell Rock Lighthouse, on the east coast of Scotland. It's Britain's oldest-working lighthouse.

The **shortest lighthouse** in Britain can be found at Berry Head in Devon, in south-west England.

14 metres

5 metres

Two **mythical liver birds** sit at the top of each tower on the historic Royal Liver building in Liverpool, north-west England.

A giant stone pineapple sits on top of a walled garden at Dunmore Park, which is an 18th century country house, near Airth in central Scotland. It is 14 metres tall and was built next to a garden that used to grow pineapples.

Baby Big Ben is the nickname of the clock tower at Pierhead, which is a 19th century building in Cardiff, Wales. It's named after the Big Ben tower in London.

Searching for a scary building to visit? Loftus Hall, in County Wexford, is said to be the most haunted building in the Republic of Ireland. Some people say it's haunted by the devil and the ghost of a young woman.

43

Britain, Ireland and books

Deciding who the best British or Irish writer is will take some time – so many great authors, playwrights and poets have come from the shores of these islands that it's difficult to choose.

The **British Library** in London is one of the world's largest in terms of the number of books, documents and articles it stores. The library was set up in 1973, and before that it was part of the British Museum.

The British Library has over **150** MILLION items.

3 MILLION new items, including books, newspapers and magazines, are added every year.

It has over **625** KILOMETRES of shelves.

It holds over **4** MILLION maps.

Famous items at the British Library:
- The *Magna Carta*
- A *Leonardo da Vinci* notebook
- The *Lindisfarne Gospels*
- *The Times* newspaper first edition (18 March 1788)
- *Beowulf* poem manuscript

Bestsellers

The Harry Potter books, penned by English writer J.K. Rowling, are the biggest-selling book series of all-time.

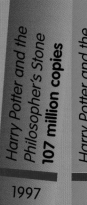

J.K. Rowling wrote some of the early Harry Potter books in coffee shops in Edinburgh.

Harry Potter and the Philosopher's Stone **107 million copies** — 1997

Harry Potter and the Chamber of Secrets **60 million copies** — 1998

Harry Potter and the Prisoner of Azkaban **60 million copies** — 1999

Harry Potter and the Goblet of Fire **55 million copies** — 2000

Harry Potter and the Order of the Phoenix **55 million copies** — 2003

Harry Potter and the Half-Blood Prince **65 million copies** — 2005

Harry Potter and the Deathly Hallows **50 million copies** — 2007

Hatchards in London is the UK's oldest bookshop. It began trading in 1797, before Charles Dickens or J.R.R. Tolkien were even born. But **Hodges Figgis** in Dublin is even older, it opened in 1768!

Written around 800 CE, ***The Book of Kells*** is an ancient religious manuscript that's on display at Trinity College, Dublin. It's considered to be Ireland's national treasure.

The historic Bodleian Library at Oxford University was established in 1602. It had strict rules about books not leaving the library. In 1645, even King Charles I was told he wasn't able to borrow a book!

Roald Dahl Day is celebrated every year on 13 September, the day the writer was born in Wales in 1916. He wrote many classic children's titles, including ...

James and the Giant Peach (1961)
Charlie and the Chocolate Factory (1964)
Danny, the Champion of the World (1975)
The BFG (1982)
Matilda (1988)

Beastly books

Frankenstein
Mary Shelley, 1818

The Hobbit
J.R.R. Tolkien, 1937

The Chronicles of Narnia
C.S. Lewis, 1950–1956

Dracula
Bram Stoker, 1897

Demon Dentist
David Walliams, 2013

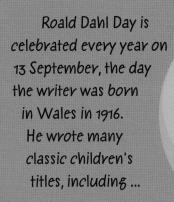

Roald Dahl was a RAF fighter pilot in the Second World War and was nearly killed in a crash landing in 1940.

Shakespeare

William Shakespeare is the most famous playwright of all time. Born in 1564 in Stratford-upon-Avon, England, his works include *Macbeth* and *Romeo and Juliet*. He wrote approximately **37 plays** and **154 sonnet** poems.

Shakespeare made up 1,700 words, such as assassin, gossip and gloomy.

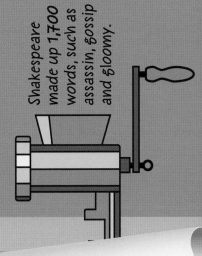

Brontë sisters

The **Brontë sisters** were born in Yorkshire between 1816 and 1820. They all wrote classic novels that have sold millions of copies.

Charlotte Brontë
1816–1855
Most famous book: Jane Eyre
Pen name: Currer Bell

Emily Brontë
1818–1848
Most famous book: Wuthering Heights
Pen name: Ellis Bell

Anne Brontë
1820–1849
Most famous book: The Tenant of Wildfell Hall
Pen name: Acton Bell

Books & letters
Lots of successful British authors are known by their initials and their surname.

J. M. Barrie – Peter Pan
A. A. Milne – Winnie-the-Pooh
E. M. Forster – A Passage to India
P.G. Wodehouse – Joy in the Morning
H. G. Wells – The War of the Worlds

English poet John Milton published his epic poem, **Paradise Lost**, in 1667. Milton's poem is about the Bible and Adam and Eve.

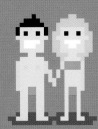

Paradise Lost was originally released in **10 books**.
The work has over **10,000** lines.

The Domesday Book was completed in **1086**. Written by scribes in medieval Latin, it was a survey of most of England and Wales to work out which land, assets and wealth people had.

Laws of the land

The laws and rules of Britain and Ireland protect and help its citizens, and allow the government to rule in the best way. But some of our laws are a little strange, to say the least …

Henry VIII was a keen sportsman and thought men should have a longbow weapon and be able to use it. The Unlawful Games Act of 1541 stated that every man aged between 17 and 60 must have a bow and regularly use it.

1839 Metropolitan Police Act

This created quite a few weird laws, which technically are still in force today …

- illegal to slide on snow or ice in the street
- against the law to carry a plank along the pavement
- illegal to beat or shake a rug in the street.

These strange laws are often said to have existed in Britain, but NEVER actually did …

- it is illegal to die in the Houses of Parliament
- it is illegal not to wear socks within **30** metres of a monarch
- it is illegal to put a stamp of the Queen upside down.

In 1571, Queen Elizabeth I's government passed a law saying that every male aged over six had to wear a **woollen cap**. Only "gentlemen", meaning men from the higher class, didn't have to.

The childhood Victorian prank of knocking on a house's door and running away was made illegal in **1847**. It was an offence to 'disturb people by ringing their doorbells or knocking at their doors'.

In 1696, a **window tax** was introduced by the government. This meant that owners of houses and buildings paid money to the government according to how many windows they had.

Records show that Floors Castle, in south-east Scotland, paid £14 and four shillings in tax for its **294** windows in **1748**. That's the same as about **£2,000** now.

In the 18th century, English law changed so that couples had to be aged **21 to marry** without their parents' permission. But in Scotland the age was 16, so many young couples went to Gretna, on the scottish border to marry instead.

In the 1640s, Oliver Cromwell's Puritan party clamped down on people celebrating Christmas and other saints and holy days. Around this time, new laws included:

- closing down the theatres
- outlawing bear-baiting, a popular but cruel animal sport
- making one day every month a fast day, where food wasn't allowed to be eaten.

King George I made a strict law to protect deer in royal parks. The Criminal Law Act of **1722** gave the death penalty to anyone who killed deer in the parks.

It is **illegal** to enter the Houses of Parliament in London wearing a suit of armour. This has been the law since 1313.

If you ever need to **move cows** through the streets, then you'll need permission from the police. In the 19th century, it became illegal to move cattle through streets between 10 am and 7 pm without permission.

The **Salmon Act** of 1986 makes it illegal for a person to handle a salmon fish in 'suspicious circumstances'.

Wonderful waterways

Many British and Irish cities and towns grew and developed because they were close to rivers and waterways. The water supply, transport, food and defence they provided were very important to people. These water sources are just as vital today.

Loch Long, in Argyll and Bute on the west coast of Scotland, is a large body of water that's about **32 kilometres** long and up to **3.2 kilometres** wide. The Royal Navy used to use it to test torpedo weapons.

3.2 kilometres

32 kilometres

Loch Ness, in the Scottish Highlands, has more fresh water than all the lakes of England and Wales combined.

The Loch Ness monster is an ancient creature rumoured to live in Loch Ness.

250,000 people visit the **Carrick-a-Rede Rope Bridge** each year in County Antrim, Northern Ireland. The bridge is 20 metres long, 30 metres high and goes across the Atlantic Ocean to the tiny Carrick-a-Rede Island.

There are 295 KILOMETRES of human-made canals in and around the city of Birmingham in central England.

The Grand Union canal is 220 KILOMETRES long. It runs from Birmingham to London.

There are **166** locks on the canal. A lock raises or lowers a canal boat travelling between stretches of water.

The Thames Barrier, in east London, opened in 1982. It was built to protect the city from flooding.

Ten big gates can be raised 15 metres

The barrier is 520 metres wide

Each gate weighs over 3,000 tonnes.

Gold, treasure and some of the royal **Crown Jewels** were allegedly lost in mud flats of the Wash, an area of water between Norfolk and Lincolnshire in east England. Apparently King John and his travelling party became stuck in the flats and lost some of their treasure.

BORE-ING RIVER FACTS

About 100 rivers around the world produce a bore – a tidal surge up the river which creates waves. Around 20 of these are in the UK.

Two-metre high waves can be made in the River Severn (Wales and west England). This is the largest tidal bore in Britain and Ireland.

1.7-metre high waves have been recorded in the River Mersey (north-west England).

The River Shannon, in the centre of the Republic of Ireland, is the longest river in the Britain and Ireland.

River Shannon, Republic of Ireland
360.5 km

River Severn, Wales and England
354 km

River Thames, England
346 km

River Tay, Scotland
188 km

River Bann, Northern Ireland
159 km

The waterfall at Pistyll Rhaeadr in north Wales is **80** METRES high. It's the highest single-drop waterfall in Britain and Ireland.

Wales is also home to **398** natural lakes and **90** human-made ones.

The **Norfolk Broads** are the only place in the UK that you can see the Fen Raft spider and the Swallowtail butterfly.

The **Pontcysyllte Aqueduct** is the largest in the UK and is found in the Dee Valley, north-east Wales. An aqueduct is a large stone bridge that carries boats or water over other waterways or valleys.

307 metres long

38 metres high

Carries **1.5** MILLION litres of water.

NORFOLK

The Norfolk Broads are a series of waterways in Norfolk and Suffolk, on the east coast of England.

More than **200** kilometres of waterways suitable for boats.

Covers an area of **303** square kilometres.

Approximately **8** MILLION people visit each year.

Ancient history

Life in Britain and Ireland was quite dangerous hundreds of years ago. Citizens were attacked by European armies and feared for their lives because of deadly diseases.

3000 BCE

The **Calanais Standing Stones** are on the Isle of Lewis in the Outer Hebrides of northern Scotland. The stones are thought to be around 5,000 years old. They are arranged in a cross shape, with the tallest stone standing 4 metres high.

Stonehenge is an ancient stone monument near the town of Amesbury in Wiltshire, south-west England.

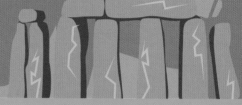

British battles

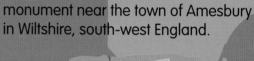

	And the winner is …
Battle of Agincourt (1415) England vs France	**England**
Bannockburn (1314) Scotland vs England	**Scotland**
Battle of Stamford Bridge (1066) Saxons vs Vikings	**Saxons**

2000 BCE

The oldest stones are thought to be **5,000** years old and date from around 3000 BCE.

There are **83** stones still at the site.

The tallest stone is **7.5** metres high.

Stonehenge could have been used as a burial ground or an area of worship.

Some of the stones were transported **250** kilometres from the Preseli Hills in Wales.

The Vikings are people who sailed from Sweden, Denmark and Norway to Britain between the 8th and 12th centuries. They fought the Anglo-Saxons and had a fierce reputation.

The first recorded Viking raid was in **793** CE on a monastery on the island of Lindisfarne, off England's north-east coast.

10,000 people lived in the important Viking city of York, or 'Jorvik' as they called it, in north-east England.

The fastest Viking longboats could reach **27** kph, which was much faster than Anglo-Saxon ships. This helped the Vikings launch surprise attacks on the coast of Britain.

Britannia is the name the Romans gave to the country. It meant 'land of tin' – the Romans wanted to capture the precious metals that Britain had.

HADRIAN'S WALL

- 15,000 soldiers built the wall
- 117.5 kilometres long
- six years to build
- 6 metres high in places and up to 3 metres wide.

£1 MILLION is the estimated value of the Galloway Hoard, which is Viking treasure found buried in Dumfries and Galloway in Scotland, in 2014.

Tynwald is the parliament of the Isle of Man, in the Irish Sea. It is over 1,000 years old and is the **oldest continually working parliament** in the world.

The Vikings were defeated at the Battle of Clontarf in 1014, near Dublin in Ireland, by an Irish army led by Brian Boru. It was the end of the Vikings' reign in Ireland.

In 122 CE, the **Emperor Hadrian** had a wall built in northern England, near where the Scottish border is now. It marked the northern end of Roman Britain and is now called Hadrian's Wall.

2000 CE

1000 CE

1000 BCE

0 CE

20,000 Roman soldiers invaded Kent, on the south coast of Britain, in 55 BCE. They were led by Roman Emperor Julius Caesar, but were **defeated by Britain's Celtic warriors**.

Before the Romans arrived, Britain had no proper roads. They built **16,000 kilometres of road**, often in straight lines because it's the quickest route between two places.

1.17 million litres of water rise each day at the **hot spa in Bath**, in Somerset in England. Hot public baths and sewers didn't exist before the Romans arrived.

Glorious parks and gardens

Brits take great pride in the beautiful flowers, gardens, parks and open spaces that are spread throughout Britain and Ireland. They make wonderful sights in any season and bring joy to millions of people, young and old.

Kew Gardens occupies **326** ACRES.

Founded in 1840, **Kew Gardens** in south-west London is one of the world's largest collections of plants.

There are more than **14,000** trees.

8.5 MILLION preserved plant species are kept in the Herbarium building. It also holds **330 species** collected by scientist Charles Darwin.

Sausage tree is the common name for the *Kigelia Africana* plant, which is grown at the Eden Project. Its fruit is used to flavour beer.

Created in Cornwall in 2001, the **Eden Project** has two huge plastic domes called 'biomes'. One of the biomes is the world's largest indoor rainforest.

There are **1,185** different species of tropical plants.

Temperatures inside the biome range from **18** degrees to a sweltering **35** degrees centigrade.

The biome is **240** metres long and **50** metres high, which is the height of about six houses.

Bananas, pineapples, rubber plants, cacao and coffee beans all grow inside.

Aberdeen in Scotland has won the **Britain in Bloom** competition 11 times. The Scottish city is known for having pretty public gardens and colourful flowers on display.

The **Chelsea Flower Show** in London is Britain's most famous flower show. Each year over 150,000 visitors see the beautiful plants on display, which come from all over the world.

There are 15 **national parks** in England, Scotland and Wales. These are large protected areas where people can enjoy the countryside, wildlife, buildings and heritage.

16.4 MILLION people visit Cumbria's Lake District every year. It's the most popular national park, filled with mountains, lakes and wildlife.

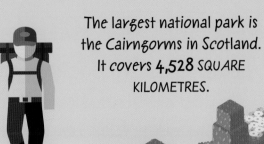

The largest national park is the Cairngorms in Scotland. It covers **4,528** SQUARE KILOMETRES.

Approximately **6 million** sunflowers grow on Vine House Farm Lincolnshire. The sunflowers are around 1.5 metres tall.

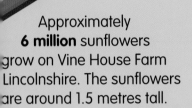

'Lampy' the garden gnome is worth **£1** MILLION. He was taken to the gardens of Lamport Hall, in Northamptonshire, from Germany in the 1840s. He is Britain's oldest surviving garden gnome.

Chatsworth House is a 16th century stately home in Derbyshire with wonderful gardens in its grounds.

Twenty full-time gardeners look after the plants and flowers.

The Emperor Water Fountain was built in **1843**. It squirts water **90** METRES into the air, which was a world record in the 1840s.

The national flower of ...

Wales = daffodil

England = Tudor rose

Scotland = Thistle

Northern Ireland = Flax flower

Republic of Ireland = Shamrock

Queen Mary's Gardens, in London's Regent's Park, opened in 1932 and has 12,000 roses planted in the gardens.

In the 16th century, **Holyrood Palace** in Edinburgh had a menagerie in its gardens. This is where exotic animals were kept, including tigers, bears, a lion and a camel.

Lay of the land

With 315,000 square kilometres of land, five countries and thousands of islands, Britain and Ireland are bursting with stacks of geographical greatness.

SHETLAND

Berwick-upon-Tweed is 555 kilometres from England's capital, London, but only 90 kilometres from Scotland's capital, Edinburgh.

555 km

90 km

The England-Scotland border = 154 km

Arthur's Seat is a famous landmark in Edinburgh. It's a 250-metre-high hill in the city's Holyrood Park.

It was formed over **2 MILLION years ago** from the remains of a volcano.

The last volcanic eruption in the UK was about 55 million years ago. The Scottish islands of Arran, Mull and Skye are the remains of volcanoes.

Most easterly
Ness Point in Lowestoft, Suffolk.

Scotland
77,933 square kilometres
14 regions

1,346 m

Ben Nevis in the Scottish Highlands is the highest mountain in Britain and Ireland. It is 1,346 metres above sea level.

Most northerly
Out Stack in the Shetland Islands, Scotland.

Most westerly
Rockall in the Atlantic Ocean, 380 kilometres from Scotland.

Most southerly
Les Minquiers Reef, Jersey, Channel Islands.

Magma from ancient Scottish volcanoes is thought to have travelled as far south as Yorkshire, England, covering 400 kilometres.

Northern Ireland
14,130 square kilometres
Six counties

*North Yorkshire is the biggest county in England at **8,654** square kilometres.*

Rutland is the smallest county in England at **382** square kilometres.

England
130,279 square kilometres
48 counties

London is the biggest city with 8.67 million residents.

Church Flatts Farm in Derbyshire is the furthest point from the sea in Britain – it's 113 kilometres away.

Wales
20,779 square kilometres
13 counties

The England-Wales border = 257 km

Cheddar Gorge is a famous valley in Somerset, south-west England.

The Cheddar Gorge cliffs are 122 metres high and go on for 4.8 kilometres.

Two caves are open to the public, with Gough's Cave going 400 metres into the rock face.

St David's, in south-west Wales, is the smallest city in Britain and Ireland with only 1,800 residents.

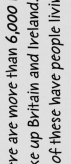

Cave Hill is a 370-metre-high hill overlooking the city of Belfast.

The Republic of Ireland -Northern Ireland border = 499 km

Republic of Ireland
70,272 square kilometres
26 counties

The lowest point in Britain and Ireland is **North Slob** in County Wexford, Republic of Ireland. It is 3 metres **below** sea level.

There are more than 6,000 islands that make up Britain and Ireland. Only about 267 of these have people living on them.

Population

Isle of Wight (English Channel)	132,000
Jersey (Channel Islands)	89,000
Isle of Mann (Irish Sea)	80,000
Anglesey (Irish Sea)	69,000
Guernsey (Channel Islands)	62,000

Famous faces

If you could choose a well-known Briton to meet, who would it be? You might need a time machine to do that, but one of the famous faces here doesn't need a time machine – he's had plenty of fun flying about in space!

Astronaut Tim Peake, born in 1972, became a world-famous Briton in 2015. He was the first British astronaut to visit the International Space Station and spent six months there. During that time he covered **125** million kilometres and orbited the Earth **3,000** times.

Emmeline Pankhurst (1858-1928) was the leader of the suffragette movement, which campaigned for women's right to vote, and decide which political parties and members of parliament would be in charge of Britain. She died just a few weeks before all women over the age of **21** were given the vote in **1928**.

Welsh footballer Gareth Bale, born in 1989, is a world record holder. Football team Real Madrid paid a then-record £**85** million for Gareth in 2013. He won the Champions League trophy with them in 2014 and 2016. He led Wales to an historic semi-final at the 2016 Euro Championship.

Born in Portsmouth, England, Isambard Kingdom Brunel (1806-1859) was a leader of engineering and industry in Britain's Industrial Revolution. His designs and knowledge led to the creation of railways, dockyards, steamships and bridges.

Sir Winston Churchill (1874–1965) was born in Blenheim Palace in Oxfordshire, England, and went on to become prime minister of the UK in the 1940s and '50s. He led Britain to victory in the Second World War. His famous hat, bow-tie and cigar are all Churchill trademarks.

Oscar Wilde (1854-1900) was a popular Irish playwright, novelist and poet. Born in Dublin, his most famous stage play was a comedy called *The Importance of Being Ernest*. He was an exciting character and challenged the strict Victorian attitudes of the late 19th century.

'The Lady with the Lamp' is the name that English nurse Florence Nightingale (1820–1910) is often remembered by. She cared for wounded soldiers during the Crimean War in the 1850s, and campaigned to raise nursing standards. She set up the nursing school at St Thomas's Hospital in London.

> **ALWAYS FORGIVE YOUR ENEMIES; NOTHING ANNOYS THEM SO MUCH**
> Oscar Wilde (1854-1900)

Big business

If you're looking to spend money on goods and services such as chocolate, teabags, coats, holidays, books and bikes, these big British companies and business will help you splash the cash.

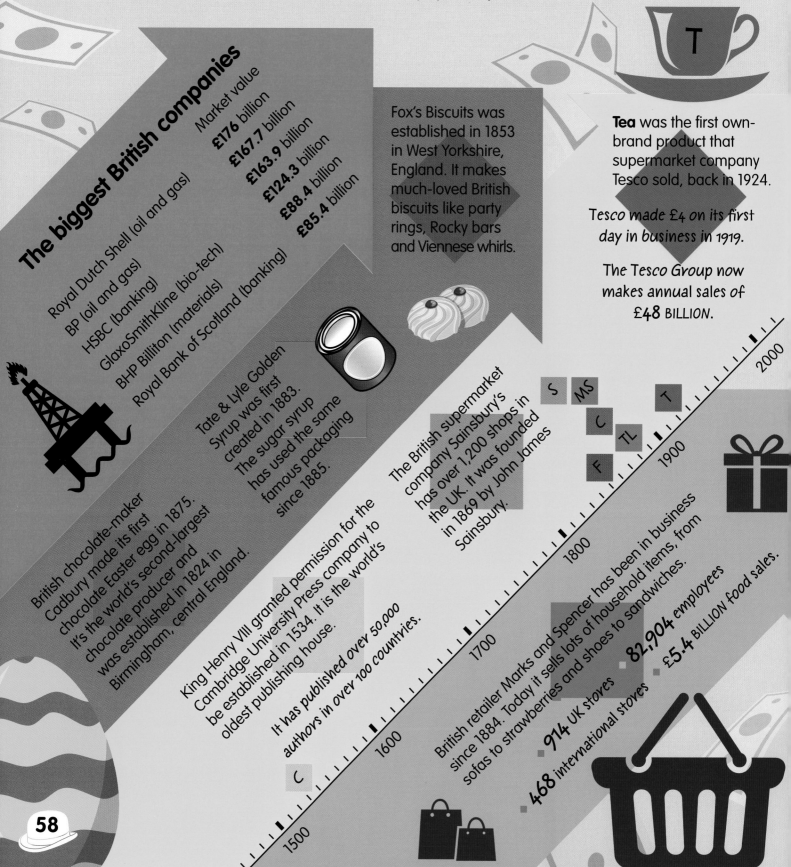

The biggest British companies

Market value

Royal Dutch Shell (oil and gas)	£176 billion
BP (oil and gas)	£167.7 billion
HSBC (banking)	£163.9 billion
GlaxoSmithKline (bio-tech)	£124.3 billion
BHP Billiton (materials)	£88.4 billion
Royal Bank of Scotland (banking)	£85.4 billion

Fox's Biscuits was established in 1853 in West Yorkshire, England. It makes much-loved British biscuits like party rings, Rocky bars and Viennese whirls.

Tea was the first own-brand product that supermarket company Tesco sold, back in 1924.

Tesco made £4 on its first day in business in 1919.

The Tesco Group now makes annual sales of £48 BILLION.

Tate & Lyle Golden Syrup was first created in 1883. The sugar syrup has used the same famous packaging since 1885.

British chocolate-maker Cadbury made its first chocolate Easter egg in 1875. It's the world's second-largest chocolate producer and was established in 1824 in Birmingham, central England.

King Henry VIII granted permission for the Cambridge University Press company to be established in 1534. It is the world's oldest publishing house.

It has published over 50,000 authors in over 100 countries.

The British supermarket company Sainsbury's has over 1,200 shops in the UK. It was founded in 1869 by John James Sainsbury.

British retailer Marks and Spencer has been in business since 1884. Today it sells lots of household items, from sofas to strawberries and shoes to sandwiches.

82,904 employees

£5.4 BILLION food sales.

914 UK stores

468 international stores

1500 1600 1700 1800 1900 2000

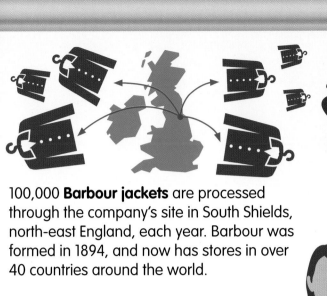

100,000 **Barbour jackets** are processed through the company's site in South Shields, north-east England, each year. Barbour was formed in 1894, and now has stores in over 40 countries around the world.

The **National Health Service** (NHS) is the biggest employer in the UK, with more than 1.5 million people. More than 1.2 million are employed by NHS England, which has …

314,966 nurses

40,584 general practitioners (GPs)

150,273 doctors

One of Ireland's most iconic companies is **Guinness**, which makes alcoholic drinks.

× 1 MILLION

More than **10** MILLION glasses of Guinness are sold every day.

Approximate **175** MILLION Pot Noodle snacks are produced in Crumlin, south Wales, each year.

The famous **gocompare.com opera singer**, who appears on the company's TV adverts, is from Wales and is called Wynne Evans.

Rival company moneysupermarket.com has its headquarters in Ewloe, north-east Wales.

Gocompare.com is based in Newport, south-east Wales.

Gearstick on the crossbar

Large seat

The **Raleigh Bicycle Company**, based in Nottinghamshire in England, released its iconic Chopper bike in 1970.

50.8 cm rear wheel   40.6 cm front wheel

On the move

The development of steam trains in the early 1800s set Britain and Ireland on course to develop one of the world's first modern transport systems, and things haven't stopped moving since …

The **RMS *Titanic* ship** was built at the Harland and Wolff shipyard in Belfast, Northern Ireland. At the time it was the world's biggest ocean-going boat.

- It was **269** METRES long and weighed **46,000** TONNES
- it cost **£5.6** MILLION to build (about **£152** MILLION today)
- it sank in the Atlantic Ocean in **1912**, on its first voyage

More than **1,500** people died.

The **M6** is the longest motorway at 373 kilometres, stretching from Catthorpe in Leicestershire to near Gretna in the Scottish borders.

The **M898** is the highest numbered motorway. It is in Renfrewshire, Scotland, and is just 0.8 kilometres long.

The **A1** is the longest numbered road in Britain and Ireland. It stretches 660 kilometres between London and Edinburgh.

The **A48(M)** is the only motorway that starts and ends in Wales. It is just 3.2 kilometres long.

1.34 BILLION passengers use the London Underground every year.

The London Underground is the **oldest underground service** in the world, opening in 1863.

There are **270 stations** on the London Underground.

The tube network is **402 kilometres** long.

The Harland and Wolff shipyard is home to the world's tallest free-standing cranes. The cranes are called Samson (106 m tall) and Goliath (96 m tall).

The world's first recorded steam locomotive journey took place between *Penydarren* and *Abercynon* in south Wales in **1804**.

The Forth Railway Bridge in east Scotland is:

- **2.46** kilometres long
- **110** metres above sea level
- weighs **53,000** tonnes
- **240,00** litres of paint were used to repaint it between **2002** and **2012**
- it was Britain's first all-steel bridge and opened in **1890**.

The TT motorbike race is held every year on the Isle of Man. The 60-kilometre course is raced in about 18 minutes.

DUNCRAIG

Duncraig railway station in the Scottish Highlands is a very small station. Fewer than 500 passengers use it each year, compared to 29 million passengers who use Glasgow Central train station in Scotland.

The longest passenger train journey in the UK, without having to change trains, is from Aberdeen in north Scotland to Penzance in Cornwall, south England. It covers **1,162 kilometres** and takes about **13.5 hours**.

The UK's first '**poo-powered**' passenger bus came into service in 2014 between Bristol and Bath in south-west England. The bus is powered by gas made by human waste.

The famous **Spaghetti Junction** motorway link in Birmingham has 559 concrete columns, covers 30 acres and uses 13,000 tonnes of steel reinforcement. It's actually called the Gravelly Hill Interchange but is nicknamed Spaghetti Junction because the roads look like spaghetti on a plate.

Britain and Ireland: more things to find

There's so much to see and do around Britain and Ireland. From stately homes and sandy beaches to magnificent monuments and awesome art galleries, here is even more information to help you visit the best bits of Britain and Ireland.

Before you go …
It's always a good idea to check the website of the place you are visiting, just to make sure it isn't closed.

Historic attractions

Battle of Hastings Abbey and Battlefield, England: www.english-heritage.org.uk/visit/places/1066-battle-of-hastings-abbey-and-battlefield

Calanais Standing Stones, Isle of Lewis, Scotland: www.callanishvisitorcentre.co.uk

Pontcysyllte Aqueduct, Wrexham, Wales: www.pontcysyllte-aqueduct.co.uk

St Patrick's Rock of Cashel, Republic of Ireland: www.heritageireland.ie/en/south-east/rockofcashel

Stonehenge, Wiltshire, England: www.english-heritage.org.uk/visit/places/stonehenge

The Giant's Causeway, Bushmills, Northern Ireland: www.giantscausewayofficialguide.com

Famous buildings

Buckingham Palace, London, England: www.royalcollection.org.uk/visit/the-state-rooms-buckingham-palace

Cardiff Castle, Cardiff, Wales: www.cardiffcastle.com

Chatsworth, Derbyshire, England: www.chatsworth.org

Edinburgh Castle, Edinburgh, Scotland: www.edinburghcastle.scot

Houses of the Oireachtas, Dublin, Republic of Ireland: www.oireachtas.ie/parliament

Titanic Belfast, Belfast, Northern Ireland: http://titanicbelfast.com/

Tower of London, London, England: www.hrp.org.uk/tower-of-london

Standing tall

Blackpool Tower, Blackpool, England: www.theblackpooltower.com

Spinnaker Tower, Portsmouth, England: www.spinnakertower.co.uk

The *Kelpies*, Falkirk, Scotland: www.thehelix.co.uk

The Shard, London, England: www.the-shard.com

The Spire, Dublin, Republic of Ireland: www.visitdublin.com/see-do

Out and about

Cheddar Gorge, Somerset, England: www.cheddargorge.co.uk

Jurassic Coast World Heritage Site, England: www.jurassiccoast.org

St Patrick's Trail, Northern Ireland: discovernorthernireland.com/about-northern-ireland/saint-patrick/saint-patricks-trail

Swansea Bay, Wales: www.visitswanseabay.com

The Kerry Way, Republic of Ireland: www.kerryway.com

The Loch Ness Centre and Exhibition, Scotland: www.lochness.com

Parks and gardens

Kew Gardens, Kew, England: www.kew.org
National Parks, Britain: www.nationalparks.gov.uk
National Parks and Wildlife Agency, Ireland: www.npws.ie/national-parks
Norfolk Broads, England: www.norfolkbroads.com
Royal Parks, England: www.royalparks.org.uk

Sports

All England Lawn Tennis Club, Wimbledon, England: www.wimbledon.com
Millennium Stadium, Cardiff, Wales: www.principalitystadium.wales
Murrayfield, Edinburgh, Scotland: www.scottishrugby.org/bt-murrayfield-stadium
Ulster Sports Museum, Ulster, Northern Ireland: www.ulstersportsmuseum.org
Wembley Stadium, London, England: www.wembleystadium.com

Full of fun

Alton Towers, England: www.altontowers.com
Dingle, Oceanworld Aquarium, Co. Kerry, Republic of Ireland: www.dingle-oceanworld.ie
Edinburgh Zoo, Edinburgh, Scotland: www.edinburghzoo.org.uk
Goquest, Dublin, Republic of Ireland: www.goquest.ie
M&D's theme park, Strathclyde Country Park, Scotland: scotlandsthemepark.com
Zip World, Bangor, Wales: www.zipworld.co.uk

Arts and culture

National Library of Ireland, Dublin, Republic of Ireland: www.nli.ie
National Museum of Scotland, Edinburgh, Scotland: www.nms.ac.uk
National Portrait Gallery, London, England: www.npg.org.uk
Tate Liverpool, Liverpool, England: www.tate.org.uk/visit/tate-liverpool
The Duncairn Centre, Belfast, Northern Ireland: www.theduncairn.com
Wales Millennium Centre, Cardiff, Wales: www.wmc.org.uk

Helpful groups

English Heritage: www.english-heritage.org.uk
England Tourist Board: www.visitengland.com
National Trust: www.nationaltrust.org.uk
Northern Ireland Tourist Board: www.discovernorthernireland.com
Republic of Ireland Tourist Board: www.discoverireland.ie
Scotland Tourist Board: www.visitscotland.com
Wales Tourist Board: www.visitwales.com

Index

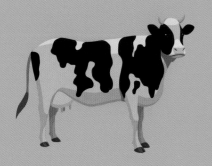